Disney's DINOSAUR

DINOSAUR-WORLD GUIDE

PUFFIN BOOKS

JOURNEY OF THE EGG

The Nesting Grounds were the safest place for the iguanodons to wait for their eggs to hatch. When an enemy attacks, one mother stands firm as the others flee. No one is going to steal *her* egg. But, when the intruder has gone, her egg has gone too, stolen by a lizard.

But this egg is a survivor, with luck on its side. The lizard drops it in a wild, rough river.

As the egg floats away, a pteranodon swoops down to pick it up and carry it across a wide sea to Lemur Island. And there the egg's journey ends – far, far away from the mother who tried to defend it.

dino Fact When dinosaurs first ruled Earth, it was a very different place. There were no continents as we know them, just one supercontinent we call Pangaea. But after millions of years, as the dinosaurs were becoming extinct, Pangaea broke up into smaller pieces. Those pieces gradually moved apart to become the continents of today.

For a long time, the dinosaurs' world was mostly green—flowers didn't appear till later. But it was a rich landscape, with tall forests of redwood, ginkgo and monkey puzzle trees, volcanoes and fern meadows.

Dinosaur eggs were smaller than you'd think. The biggest found so far is less than 30 centimetres long, and some are only 20 centimetres. Unlike the brittle eggs of modern birds, they had a thick leathery shell. They may have been left to hatch in the heat of the sun, or were covered with sand.

The biggest meat eaters ate other dinosaurs. Others ate things like large insects and lizards. Ferns, conifers and cycads (they looked something like palm trees) were all eaten by plant eaters. Some had to swallow stones to help to digest their food.

ALADAR

From the moment he hatches, Dinosaur's iguanodon hero, Aladar, lives with a lemur family. So he grows up gentle and kind, in spite of his huge size.

When he first meets other iguanodons, Aladar is amazed. And he falls in love with Neera, sister of the Herd's brutal leader, Kron.

But Aladar soon realises that Kron's ideas are very different from his own. The leader leaves the old and feeble to fall prey to their carnotaur enemies. He never tries to help them.

Aladar's gentleness hides an inner strength. He does not want to challenge Kron, but in the end he has no choice ...

dino Fact

There were two main types of dinosaurs. Plant eaters fed on conifers and ferns, and meat eaters ate other dinosaurs. The first plant eaters went on all fours. Then a new kind evolved: two footed plant eaters. Their large bellies were slung between their hind legs. This meant they could also stand upright, as the meat eaters did.

Iguanodons could
be 10 metres long and
weighed about 7 tonnes. They
were two footed plant eaters.
Members of this group are called
ornithopods, which means
'bird-footed'. The first fossilised
footprints found showed a three
toed foot, like that of a bird.
So for a while, the footprints
were thought to be
those of a bird.

Iguanodons had hands
quite like a human's.
But where we have
thumbs, they had
hard sharp spurs
that could be used
as weapons.

As well as having bird feet, iguanodons
belong to the Ornithischian group.
This means 'bird-hipped'. The iguanodon's
hip bones were side by side, pointing in
the same direction, like those of a bird.

PLIO AND YAR

Plio rules the lemurs in her own wise fashion. The lemurs know she is both fair and kind, so her advice is in great demand.

When Aladar hatches from his egg, she protects him from harm. She takes him into the family, adopting him as one of her own.

Her warm, motherly nature teaches Aladar the value of family life and of working together – something he never forgets.

Yar, Plio's father, used to rule the lemur clan. Since he is officially retired, he has to take a back seat these days. But this doesn't stop him from sticking his nose into everyone's business whenever he feels like it.

Although he can sound gruff and harsh, the lemurs all know he is probably the biggest softie on Lemur Island!

dino Fact Fossils found of the first lemurs that appeared on Earth show there were several kinds. Some types died out – there was once a species of lemur larger than an adult male gorilla. Others continued in tropical forests and there are many different kinds on the island of Madagascar.

Along with humans and monkeys, lemurs are part of the group of mammals called primates. They are related to monkeys, but are regarded as a separate species. They range in size from 13 cm up to 60 cm. Lemurs have a keen sense of smell, and woolly fur.

The lemurs that live on Madagascar are found nowhere else on Earth.

SURI

Suri is Plio's daughter, a sparkling young female full of energy. She loves Aladar, and thinks it's great to have a large dinosaur as her older brother.

But when their island home is destroyed, Suri loses some of her confidence. Their new world is big and frightening. She turns to her mother as her only security, and clings to her.

Once they're all safe in the Nesting Grounds, Suri gradually becomes her old feisty self again.

dino Fact
Some lemurs are in danger of becoming extinct. This is because their habitats are being destroyed, and they are being hunted or trapped by humans. One species that is critically endangered is Sclater's black lemur. It is the only type of lemur with blue eyes.

ZINI

Zini is Aladar's best friend. He is a young lemur with a high opinion of himself. He's sure he is a great hit with the ladies. They don't always agree, but he doesn't let that get him down.

He's a lemur who's always ready to lend a hand when it's needed. Sadly, Zini is a bit clumsy, and from time to time this gets him into trouble ...

dino Fact There are more mouse lemurs than any other kind on the island of Madagascar. These tiny creatures eat flowers, fruit and leaves as well as small animals such as chameleons and frogs. They also eat tree gum and sap. The female usually has twins, carrying her babies in her mouth for the first three weeks.

The best known of all lemurs is the ring-tailed lemur. These lemurs live in groups of 3–20, and use their long bushy tails to signal to one another.

COMETS AND FIREBALLS

The lemurs love their island, and so does their big friend Aladar. It has everything, and it's a great place to grow up. They all think life there will go on for ever, and nothing can spoil it.

Then one terrible day, a comet crosses the sky and crashes to Earth. It hurls a fireball at the little island, and suddenly everything changes.

As the fireball approaches the island, Aladar rushes the lemurs to safety on the mainland. And from there, they look back to see Lemur Island in flames. Their home is no more ...

dino Fact Fireballs can be one of two things. They can be large, hot fires, often formed of burning gases. Or they can be shooting stars – that is, the bright flash of light as a meteor crosses the sky.

Comets are bright objects in space trailing long tails made of dust and gases. Most famous of all is Halley's Comet, which can only be seen from Earth once every seventy-six years or so, when it is at its closest.

Meteors and meteorites are lumps of stone, iron or carbon material. Meteors burn up completely before they get to Earth. Meteorites actually reach the Earth.

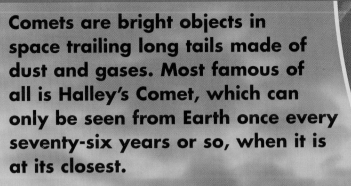

Meteorites make round holes when they hit Earth, and those holes can be huge. The Meteor Crater in Arizona is over a kilometre across. (It should really be called Meteorite Crater, of course, but was named before that distinction was made.)

A fire storm is something no one wants to see. It's a huge fire that spreads fast, feeding itself by the high winds it creates. Luckily they don't happen often, because they can only be left to burn themselves out. Not even the most modern firefighting methods can control a fire storm.

NESTING GROUNDS

The dinosaurs have their own Nesting Grounds, where they make their way each year. The Herd looks forward to peace and safety in its own special place. They all know the way so well they could get there blindfold.

But this year is different. A fireball flew along the route before them, and everything died. There's little food, and the lake has dried up.

Their leader Kron bullies them into hurrying, but the Herd is losing hope. Will they ever get there?

dino Fact When herds were on the move, they still took care of their young. Fossil tracks found show that smaller dinosaurs travelled in the middle of the herd, with the larger ones patrolling the edges.

The first fossil dinosaur nests were discovered in the Gobi Desert in 1922. Since then, nests have been found all over the world. Some just have eggs, others have hatchlings as well as eggs.

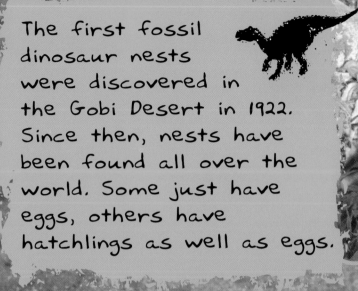

Danger could threaten the eggs even when they were well guarded. One unusual dinosaur specialised in stealing eggs – the oviraptor (its name means 'egg thief'). It was under 2 metres long, with big jaws. It had no teeth, but it had two sharp points in the roof of its mouth.

Some dinosaurs looked after their babies in the way birds do. They even brought them food as birds do. One mother who did this was the two footed plant eater Maiasaura.

SURVIVAL AND EXTINCTION

dino Fact Few people would call dinosaurs beautiful. But those enormous beasts have been fuelling our imaginations for nearly two hundred years. What were they like, what colour were they, how did they behave, were they cold-blooded – and the biggest question of all, why are there none left?

By now, we know quite a lot. They appeared on Earth about 228 million years ago, and ruled for about 160 million years.

Why, then, did they become extinct 65 million years ago? We have no real answers, only theories.

The Theories

Theories are not facts. They are only what we think may be the case.

One theory is that a star exploded near Earth, sending out cosmic rays (they contain tiny particles) that killed all life. Another is that the climate cooled down gradually. Plant life changed and could no longer support plant eating dinosaurs, which meant the meat eaters had no food either.

But many scientists now believe that it could have been some natural disaster, such as a comet or huge asteroid colliding with Earth. Dust and steam from this could have blanketed the planet for years, keeping the sun's heat out. So, again, plants and animals would die.

> The word 'dinosaur' did not come into the English language until 1841. It was made up by a British scientist, Sir Richard Owen, and means 'terrible lizard'. About 250 different kinds of dinosaur fossils have been found so far, but it is believed that hundreds may be waiting to be discovered.

VELOCIRAPTORS

The Herd is not short of enemies. As well as the carnotaurs, the velociraptors are an ever-present threat.

Kron knows they are at least as bloodthirsty as the carnotaurs, and they have fearsome claws. His scouts must be on the alert every minute of every day. And the Herd must keep moving. They must get to the Nesting Grounds – and safety – as fast as possible.

dino Fact

Velociraptors were about 1.8 metres long, about the same size as a German Shepherd dog. They were very quick (as their name in fact suggests – it means 'fast thief'). They had long, narrow heads, and the same kind of large claw on their second toes that the deinonychus had.

In 1984, a British farmer discovered yet another similar claw. It was 31cm long – about three times as big as the other two!

Velociraptors had surprisingly few teeth—only about 30 in each jaw. But as teeth go, they were wickedly efficient, with saw-edges both front and back.

In the 1920s, it was believed that man's ancestors might have come from Asia. So four expeditions went to the Gobi Desert in Mongolia to find out. They didn't find any human remains—but they did find fossils of five dinosaurs previously unknown to science. One of these was a velociraptor.

There was a really spectacular find in Mongolia in 1971. Two dinosaurs were found locked together in mortal combat. A velociraptor had all four feet gripped round the skull of its victim, a protoceratops. No one knows why they died together in this way.

When we think of fossils, we think of bones and skeletons. But they can be teeth, skin, eggs, footprints, and even droppings! The best places to find them are deserts or cliffs.

EEMA

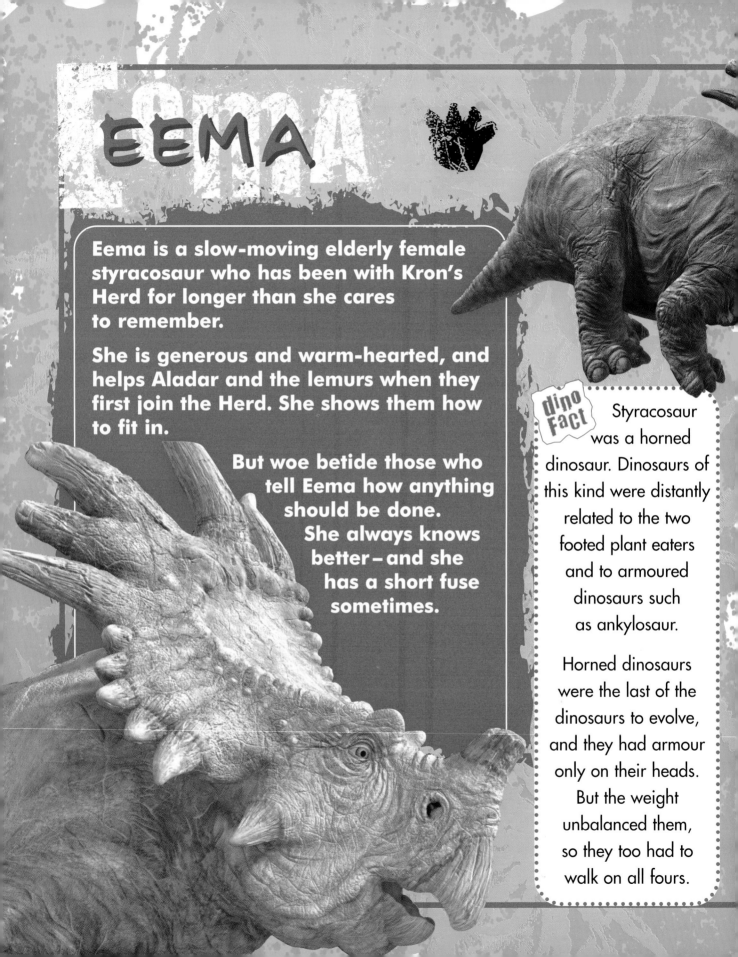

Eema is a slow-moving elderly female styracosaur who has been with Kron's Herd for longer than she cares to remember.

She is generous and warm-hearted, and helps Aladar and the lemurs when they first join the Herd. She shows them how to fit in.

But woe betide those who tell Eema how anything should be done. She always knows better – and she has a short fuse sometimes.

dino Fact Styracosaur was a horned dinosaur. Dinosaurs of this kind were distantly related to the two footed plant eaters and to armoured dinosaurs such as ankylosaur.

Horned dinosaurs were the last of the dinosaurs to evolve, and they had armour only on their heads. But the weight unbalanced them, so they too had to walk on all fours.

Styracosaurs were 5.5 metres long – about the size of a modern hippopotamus. Their teeth were extremely sharp – perhaps to chew through tough palm fronds.

The word styracosaur means 'spiked reptile'. It had a horn on its nose, and long fearsome spikes on its neck frill.

Fossil tracks show that many dinosaurs such as styracosaurs and pachyrhinosaurs travelled in herds. They may also have formed defensive circles, with the females and young inside. The armoured heads would form an almost impenetrable hedge against attack.

The pachyrhinosaur was also a horned dinosaur – but it didn't have a real horn. Instead, it had a thick heavy battering ram on its nose.

BAYLENE

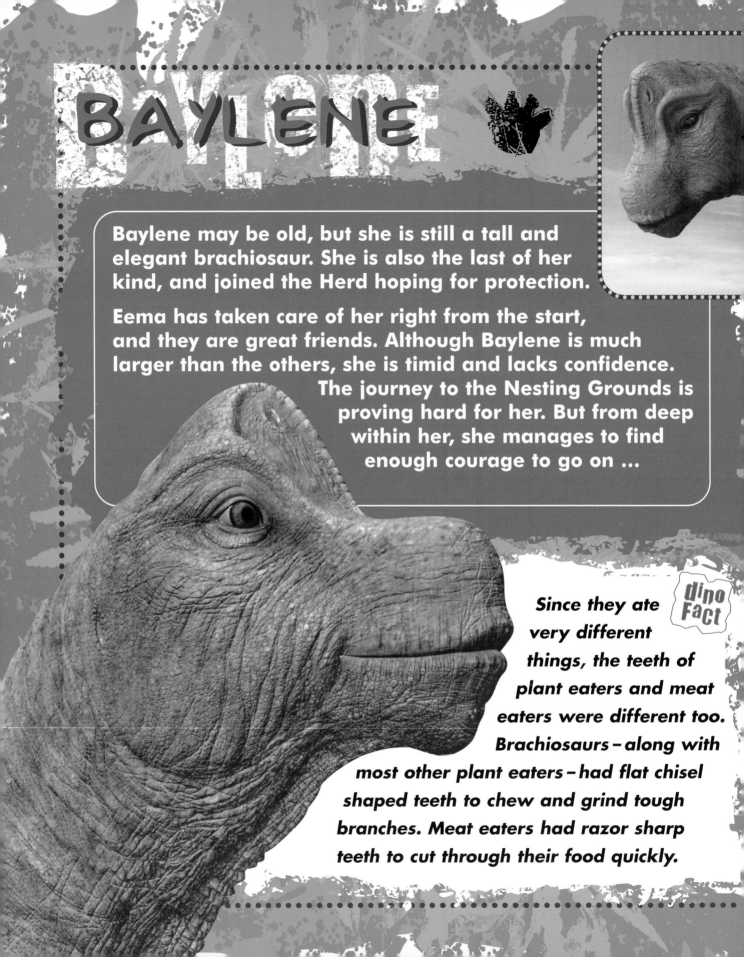

Baylene may be old, but she is still a tall and elegant brachiosaur. She is also the last of her kind, and joined the Herd hoping for protection.

Eema has taken care of her right from the start, and they are great friends. Although Baylene is much larger than the others, she is timid and lacks confidence. The journey to the Nesting Grounds is proving hard for her. But from deep within her, she manages to find enough courage to go on ...

dino Fact

Since they ate very different things, the teeth of plant eaters and meat eaters were different too. Brachiosaurs – along with most other plant eaters – had flat chisel shaped teeth to chew and grind tough branches. Meat eaters had razor sharp teeth to cut through their food quickly.

Just when the iguanodons were emerging, the brachiosaurs were becoming extinct. They were long necked plant eaters that went on all fours, using their long necks to feed from high branches.

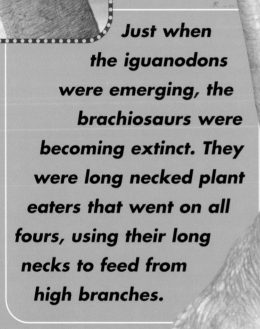

One of the biggest land animals ever, brachiosaur weighed in at over 50 tonnes. It stood 12 metres tall, and could be up to 25 metres long. There were big nostrils on top of its head, but no one knows exactly what these were for. An even taller dinosaur was the Ultrasaurus. It stood 18 metres high!

Brachiosaur means 'arm reptile'. They were called this because their front legs were longer than their hind legs. Their feet had five toes, with a single claw.

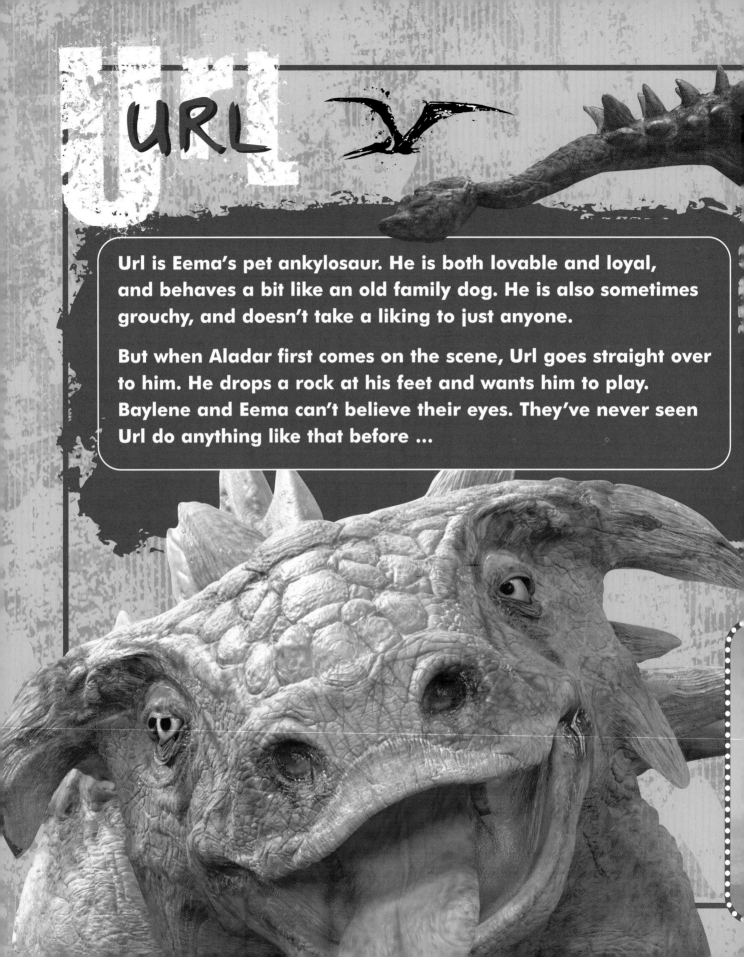

URL

Url is Eema's pet ankylosaur. He is both lovable and loyal, and behaves a bit like an old family dog. He is also sometimes grouchy, and doesn't take a liking to just anyone.

But when Aladar first comes on the scene, Url goes straight over to him. He drops a rock at his feet and wants him to play. Baylene and Eema can't believe their eyes. They've never seen Url do anything like that before ...

The name ankylosaur means 'stiff lizard'. Ankylosaurs were plant eating dinosaurs with armour on their backs to protect them from the meat eaters. They had strong, bony heads, and even their eyelids were armoured.

Although ankylosaurs would only fight if attacked, some had weapons such as big tail-clubs, or spines along their sides. One called Mymoorapelta had blades on its tail. It lived in North America.

Their armour made the ankylosaurs really heavy – too heavy to walk upright. They had to walk on all fours.

Most ankylosaurs were about 5 metres long, but there were several different kinds. The smallest one was about the size of a sheep. The largest ankylosaur was over 7 metres long and lived in North America.

Nearly all the ankylosaur fossils found in most parts of the world were upside down. They may have lived on swampy land, where their weight would have turned them over on their backs as they sank down through the mud.

KRON

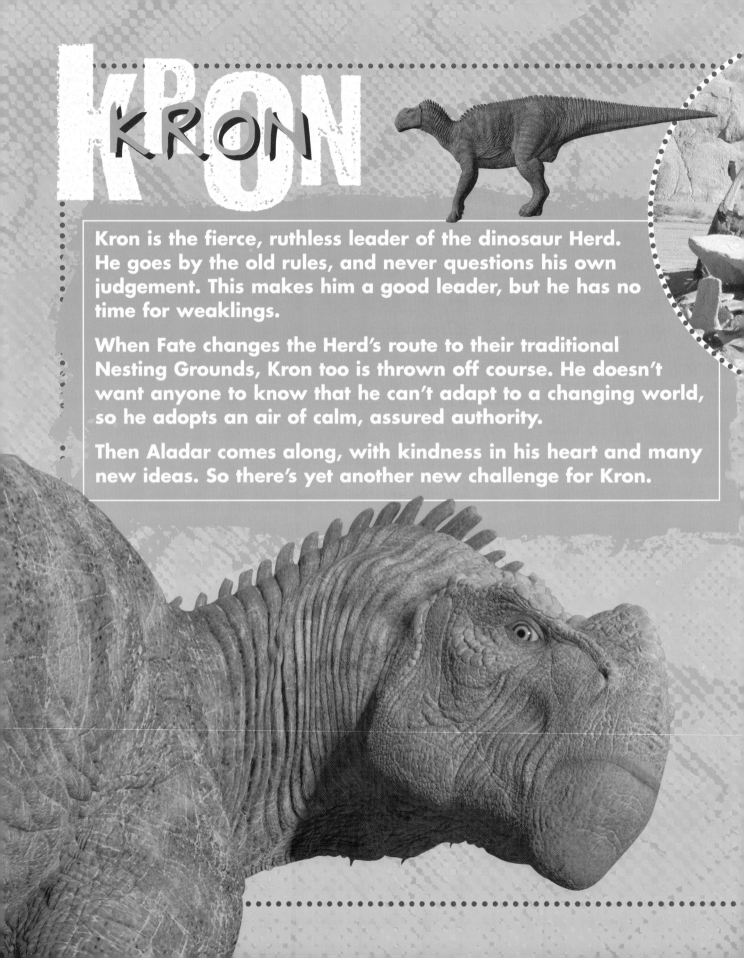

Kron is the fierce, ruthless leader of the dinosaur Herd. He goes by the old rules, and never questions his own judgement. This makes him a good leader, but he has no time for weaklings.

When Fate changes the Herd's route to their traditional Nesting Grounds, Kron too is thrown off course. He doesn't want anyone to know that he can't adapt to a changing world, so he adopts an air of calm, assured authority.

Then Aladar comes along, with kindness in his heart and many new ideas. So there's yet another new challenge for Kron.

Until the beginning of the 19th century, no one had even heard of dinosaurs. But before the end of that century, fossilised bones had been found of nearly all the different kinds. The first iguanodon bones and teeth were discovered by a palaeontologist called Dr Gideon Mantell in the 1820s. He did not realise however that it walked upright. He thought it was a lizard, because the teeth were like those of a present-day iguana, only bigger. So he called it iguanodon-iguan from a Mexican lizard, odon meaning tooth.

In spite of their size and weight, iguanodons could move quite fast, lifting their tails off the ground as they ran.

We know more about iguanodons than other dinosaurs because so many have been found. Fifty years after Dr Mantell's first find, 23 fossilised skeletons were dug up in Belgium – and they were all iguanodons.

Palaeontologists are scientists who study fossils and early life on Earth. Sometimes they make mistakes – iguanodons were once thought to have horns on their noses. And the thumbs on their hands were believed to be horns. But as time goes on, such mistakes are corrected. More and more is becoming known about the great beasts that once reigned supreme for millions and millions of years.

NEERA

Neera is just as strong-minded as her brother Kron, and she also shares his belief in traditional values.

But those values are turned upside down when she meets Aladar. She finds his kind, gentle ways unusual and appealing.

Neera does not want to defy her brother and follow Aladar. But at last she has to face the truth. The old ways are not always the best ...

dino Fact

Two footed dinosaurs began to roam the world about 200 million years ago, in the Triassic period. Iguanodons evolved much later – about 100 million years ago, in the Cretaceous period.

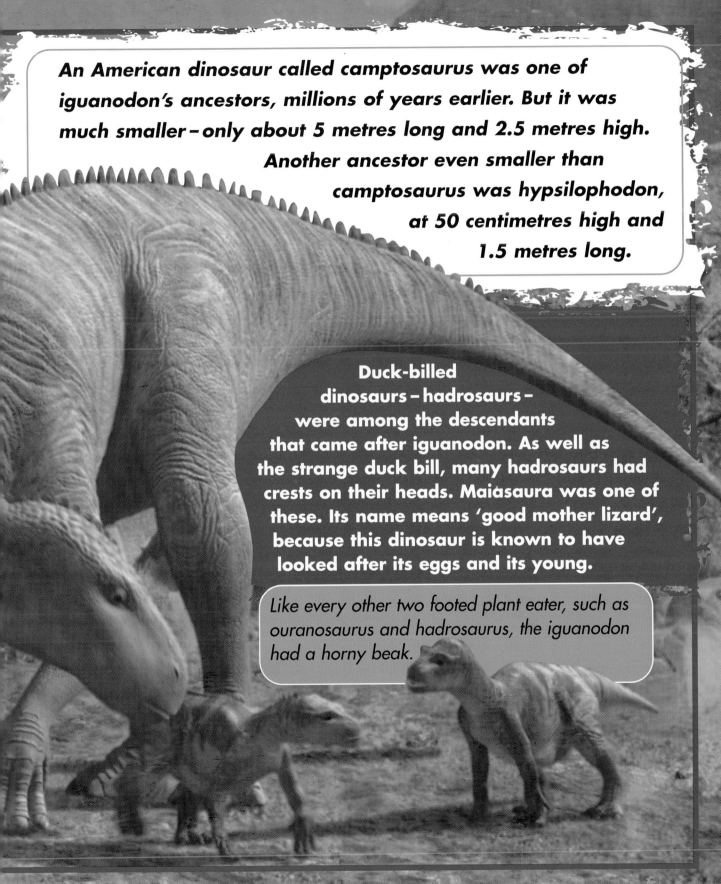

An American dinosaur called camptosaurus was one of iguanodon's ancestors, millions of years earlier. But it was much smaller – only about 5 metres long and 2.5 metres high. Another ancestor even smaller than camptosaurus was hypsilophodon, at 50 centimetres high and 1.5 metres long.

Duck-billed dinosaurs – hadrosaurs – were among the descendants that came after iguanodon. As well as the strange duck bill, many hadrosaurs had crests on their heads. Maiasaura was one of these. Its name means 'good mother lizard', because this dinosaur is known to have looked after its eggs and its young.

Like every other two footed plant eater, such as ouranosaurus and hadrosaurus, the iguanodon had a horny beak.

27

CARNOTAURS

Very few things frighten Aladar – or Kron, for that matter. But they both know just how terrifying the carnotaur hunters are.

These enemies are vicious meat eaters, preying on other dinosaurs. And they stalk the Herd, grasping every opportunity to attack.

Kron has scouts on the move behind the Herd to keep him informed of danger. Later, he fights a carnotaur, and loses his life. Aladar risks his life as well, but is finally triumphant.

dino Fact Meat eaters were not large. Compsognathus was the smallest of all. It was about as big as a chicken!

Carnotaurs lived in South America. They had horns very like a bull.

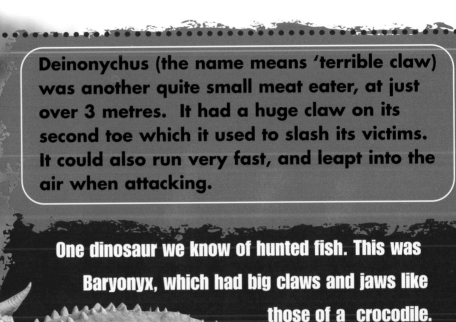

Deinonychus (the name means 'terrible claw) was another quite small meat eater, at just over 3 metres. It had a huge claw on its second toe which it used to slash its victims. It could also run very fast, and leapt into the air when attacking.

One dinosaur we know of hunted fish. This was Baryonyx, which had big claws and jaws like those of a crocodile.

In one way or another – armour, or size and weight – the plant eaters had their own defences. They needed them, because hungry meat eaters were always on the prowl. They were fast and vicious, with sharp teeth and long jaws. Biggest of all was Tyrannosaurus, at 12 metres long. It had long hind legs and stood upright, with a heavy tail to balance its body. Its terrible teeth could be as long as 15 centimetres or more. And as well as being sharp, they were saw-edged, something like the steak knives we use today.

THE MAKING OF

Nowadays, everyone knows what dinosaurs were, and what their world was like.

Blending computer animation and live action, Disney's DINOSAUR film breathes life into that strange primeval world. From the largest character to the smallest, from the youngest to the oldest, they all have their own ideas and feelings.

Their story is one of a struggle for survival, and also hope. Looking after one another is the only way they can win through – and they do!

An idea takes shape ...

And develops ...

And goes live ...

Baylene gets stuck – and finds water for the Herd

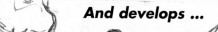

A FABULOUS FILM

Science takes a hand: learning how faces work. It's got to be right.

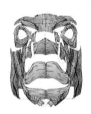

Making them move – the arrows show where animation controls were added to make the dinosaurs move naturally.

It's Url – from start to finish

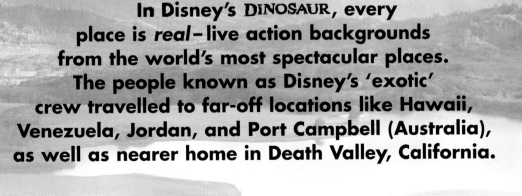

In Disney's DINOSAUR, every place is *real* – live action backgrounds from the world's most spectacular places. The people known as Disney's 'exotic' crew travelled to far-off locations like Hawaii, Venezuela, Jordan, and Port Campbell (Australia), as well as nearer home in Death Valley, California.

DO YOU KNOW?

1 Which was the fiercest dinosaur?

2 Which was the smallest dinosaur?

3 Which dinosaurs had armoured eyelids?

4 Which lemur has blue eyes?

5 Which island is famous for lemurs?

6 What does oviraptor mean?

7 Are dinosaur eggs huge?

8 Which dinosaur was a good mother?

9 Did the very biggest dinosaur eat meat or plants?

10 When were the first dinosaur fossils found?

The answers are all in this book